Sports Illustrated
ICE HOCKEY

The Sports Illustrated Library

BOOKS ON TEAM SPORTS

Baseball	Curling: Techniques and Strategy	Ice Hockey
Basketball	Football: Defense	Soccer
	Football: Offense	Volleyball

BOOKS ON INDIVIDUAL SPORTS

Badminton	Horseback Riding	Table Tennis
Fly Fishing	Skiing	Tennis
Golf	Squash	Track and Field: Running Events

BOOKS ON WATER SPORTS

Powerboating	Small Boat Sailing
Skin Diving and Snorkeling	Swimming and Diving

SPECIAL BOOKS

Dog Training	Training with Weights
Safe Driving	

Sports Illustrated
ICE HOCKEY

By MARK MULVOY
and the Editors of
Sports Illustrated

Illustrations by
Isa Barnett

J. B. LIPPINCOTT COMPANY

Philadelphia and New York

ISBN-0-397-00835-X Cloth Edition
ISBN-0-397-00836-8 Paper Edition
Copyright © 1971 by Time, Inc.
All rights reserved
Sixth Printing
Printed in the United States of America
Library of Congress Catalog Card No.: 78–156366

Photographs from *Sports Illustrated*, © Time, Inc.
Cover photograph by Al Freni
Photograph by Richard Raphael: page 8
Photographs by Walter Iooss, Jr.: pages 22 and 38
Photographs by Tony Triolo: pages 28, 58, 66 and 82

Contents

1
The Game

HOCKEY is the fastest team sport in the world and the most difficult of all games to play and watch. Performing on skates and wearing a dozen pieces of protective equipment, the hockey player must move with his head up at all times to avoid body checks and errant sticks, and still manage to control the little black puck at the end of his own stick. He must keep his balance—and his composure too—despite severe body contact, and he must execute all of hockey's complicated maneuvers without breaking his skating stride. Clearly, the hockey player's job is a difficult one.

For example, what about the goaltenders, those lonely men who guard the 4-foot-by-6-foot cages at opposite ends of the hockey rink and who receive all the blame for a defeat but rarely any of the credit for a victory? Goaltenders know that at any second a player may skate in all alone and slap that hard, cold puck at them from 20 or 25 feet away at speeds of 100 miles an hour and better.

It is the speed and the continuous movement on ice that make the player's and the spectator's job a demanding one.

The fan is rewarded for alertness and concentration, penalized for inattention and mental laziness. At a hockey game, spectators must keep their eyes on the puck. That's where the action is. One important reminder for all spectators: never throw anything onto the ice during the course of a game. Many promising hockey careers have been destroyed or imperiled because a thoughtless fan tossed a penny or a bottle cap or a pin or some other small object onto the rink, and in the heat of competition a player skated over it, lost his balance and slammed uncontrollably into the boards.

THE RINK

Hockey is played on an ice surface called a "rink." The standard rink is 200 feet long and 85 feet wide. The rink is surrounded by boards that extend some 43 inches above the level of the ice. All rinks should have either glass or wire protective screens above the boards to prevent pucks from flying into the crowd. Ten feet from each end of the rink are the goal posts and the nets. The vertical posts are 4 feet high; the horizontal post is 6 feet in length. A 2-inch red line runs between the vertical goal posts and extends across the rink and up the side of the boards. A goal is scored only when the puck (a vulcanized rubber disk, frozen before the game, that is 1 inch thick, 3 inches in diameter and weighs between 5½ and 6 ounces) completely crosses that red line between the goal posts and enters the cage. The rectangular area marked in front of the goal is called the "crease." It belongs to the goaltender. No opposing player is permitted to enter the crease at any time; if he does, and if his team happens to score a goal at the same time, then the goal is disallowed. Goaltenders have discovered that not-so-gentle taps on the ankles discourage rivals from standing around near the crease.

The rink is divided into three zones—defensive, neutral, and attacking—by two blue lines, each exactly 1 foot wide;

they are drawn 60 feet from the goal lines at both ends of the rink. Like the goal lines, they extend completely across the rink and up the boards. In effect, there are two defensive zones and two attacking zones; the defensive zone for one team is the attacking zone for the other, and vice versa. For example, the area inside one blue line—that is, the area between the blue line and the closer end of the rink—is the defensive zone for Team A, since that team is attempting to defend the goal there, and it also is the attacking zone for Team B, since that team is attempting to score on the goal there.

THE RINK

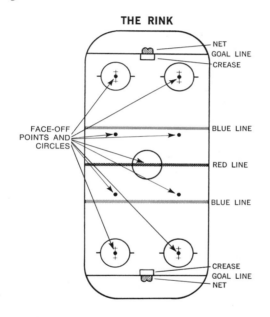

The area between the blue lines is called the neutral zone or center ice; it is bisected by a red line which is, like the blue lines, 12 inches wide and which extends across the ice and up the boards.

Also drawn on the ice are five faceoff circles, each with a radius of 15 feet, and four more red faceoff drop areas. Faceoffs (two rival players trying to control the puck when it is dropped by an official) occur every time there is a stoppage of play.

There is one faceoff circle at center ice where play begins at the start of a period or after a goal has been scored. There also are two faceoff circles in each of the other zones. Play resumes there when the defensive team has somehow managed to stop play. The four faceoff drop areas are all in the neutral zone. Two of them are drawn 5 feet from each blue line and exactly 44 feet apart. Play begins there generally following such violations as off sides.

THE PLAYERS

At the start of a game, each team is permitted to send six skaters onto the ice. They are a goaltender, two defensemen and three forwards: a right wing, a center and a left wing. Excluding the goaltenders, who play the entire game, these players usually stay on the ice for about two minutes before they are replaced by a new shift. Forwards normally rotate in three shifts; that is, a team usually skates three forward lines. Defensemen, though, rotate every other shift because most teams carry only two defensive teams. Player changes in hockey are done "on the fly." That is, there is no stoppage of play while a team makes substitutions. Changing on the fly is a tricky business: often a team finds itself with an extra skater on the ice because of a mixup during the line change—and then it is assessed a 2-minute penalty for playing with too many skaters on the ice.

There is, however, a foolproof way for all teams to effect their line changes: players should substitute by position. For example, the right wing should skate onto the ice only when the right wing he is replacing has skated to the bench. The center replaces the center, the left defenseman replaces the other left defenseman, and so on. This eliminates confusion and prevents needless penalties. Also, line changes should be made only when a team is moving into the attacking zone or with play continuing harmlessly around center ice. Teams should never change players when play is in their defensive zone; if they do, the attacking team will have a momentary player advantage—and that could be disastrous.

THE RULES

The rules of hockey are relatively simple to understand, but in the course of action it's difficult to detect violations of these rules that cause officials to blow their whistles and halt the play. There really are only two technical rules that players and spectators must understand in order to play and appreciate the game. They are "off sides" and "icing."

    1. Off Sides. This rule has two aspects:
        A. Any time a player passes the puck across two lines (blue and red) to a teammate, then the play is off sides and the referee whistles the action dead. He orders a faceoff at the originating point of the off-sides pass.

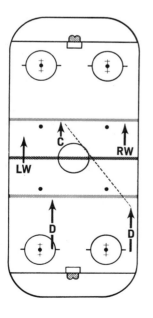

Any time a player passes the puck over two lines to a teammate, the play itself is off sides. See text for other off-sides situations.

B. Any time an attacking player precedes the puck across the blue line and into the attacking zone, then he is off side and the referee whistles the play dead. He calls for a faceoff usually in one of the drop areas just outside the blue line.

(The position of a player's skates—not his stick— determines the off-sides violation. A player is off side only when *both* his skates have crossed the outer edge of the red or blue line involved in the play. In other words, a player can straddle the involved line—keeping one skate in a legal on-sides position—and not be off sides.)

2. Icing. When a team shoots the puck from its half of the ice all the way down the other end of the ice and across the red goal line, and a rival player—excluding the goaltender—touches the puck first, then the referee whistles "icing." He calls the puck back and orders a faceoff in one of the circles near the goaltender of the team that "iced" the puck. Icing, however, is permitted when a team is playing short-handed, trying to kill a penalty.

When a player shoots the puck over the red line, the blue line and then the goal line and a rival player (except the goaltender) touches it first, "icing" is called.

⊗ —DEFENSIVE PLAYER
× —GOALIE

14

PENALTIES

Penalties are almost inescapable during a hockey game; however, many of them result from unnecessary, often irrational moves by a player who has just been beaten somehow by his opponent, and the player thinks he must retaliate —even though he does it illegally.

These are the penalties most frequently called in a hockey game:

1. *Holding:* generally a stupid penalty to take. Grabbing an opponent momentarily rarely incurs a penalty, but doing it obviously and for any length of time will not go unpunished. The best defensemen in hockey are masters at tying up rival players without making spectacles of it.

2. *Tripping:* a judgment penalty, usually called only when the trip itself is flagrant and/or intentional. Tripping is more apt to be called when the play is in the attacking zone than when it is out at center ice, where the action is not so crucial.

Tripping

3. *Hooking*: a dangerous act in which the blade of the hockey stick is hooked into the body or the arms of another player.

Hooking

4. *Slashing*: a penalty called when a player hits another player with the stick, usually in a fit of temper and in retaliation. The stick itself does not need to make contact, if there was "intent to injure."

5. *Interference*: a marginal penalty that occurs when a player hinders a rival not directly involved in the play. It is a maneuver that gains nothing for the offender. Also, players who are interfered with oftentimes suffer severe injuries, since they do not expect to be hit. Generally, interference is permitted close to the net, where defensemen and attacking players try to occupy the same area.

16

6. *Charging:* a penalty called when a player makes a body check that is not a normal outgrowth of the action but requires three or four deliberate steps toward the victim.

7. *Spearing:* the most serious of all transgressions, calling for an automatic 5-minute penalty. As the term suggests, spearing is thrusting the blade of your stick at an opponent —particularly at his stomach.

8. *Elbowing:* a penalty for a check made with the arms or elbows instead of the body.

Elbowing

9. *High Sticking:* carrying your stick above shoulder level when moving into a direct confrontation with a rival.

17

10. *Cross Checking:* a variation of high sticking. This time a player holds his stick at each end and rams it at another player.

Cross Checking

There also are penalties for such infractions as deliberately attempting to injure an opponent, delaying the game, playing with a broken stick, handling the puck, throwing a stick at another player and, as mentioned before, playing with too many players on the ice.

Major penalties are 5 minutes long, and are imposed when two players resort to fisticuffs instead of hockey, or when a player cuts his opponent, drawing blood, while committing an illegal act. Misconduct penalties—called when a player uses abusive language in discussion with an official—are for 10 minutes, but the offender's team does not have to play a man short for the 10 minutes; the player given the misconduct penalty may not play for 10 minutes.

Certain penalties result in penalty shots: a player is given

18

the puck at center ice and allowed to skate in alone on the goaltender, attempting any single shot in an effort to score a goal. Penalty-shot situations result from a number of infractions. For instance, if a player breaks in alone on the goaltender, then is interfered with illegally from behind and cannot get his shot away, he is given a penalty shot. Also, if a defending player other than the goaltender handles the puck in the crease, the attacking team is given a penalty shot.

THE EQUIPMENT

The two basic pieces of equipment for a hockey player are, naturally, his skates and his stick. They will be discussed in detail in following chapters. There are, however, a number of other pieces of gear each player must wear to protect himself against the risky elements that make up the game of hockey. Goaltenders have their own special equipment; their regalia is discussed in the goaltender's section later in the book. All other hockey players should skate onto the ice only when wearing all the following pieces of equipment:

1. Hockey Gloves. They must fit snugly. The thumb is the most important consideration: there must be extra-hard protection around the thumb area, since that's the spot most frequently hit by rival sticks during a game. Gloves must also have a padded area covering the wrists. The palms should be as thin as possible so that the player can get maximum feel from his stick.

2. Shin Guards. Defensemen must have shin guards with extra protection around the knees, since they are called upon to block shots. Forwards should have lightweight shin guards that offer enough protection against pucks but do not hinder skating.

3. Elbow Pads. The elbows oftentimes are the first part of a player's body to hit the boards following a check; therefore, lightweight elbow pads are a must.

4. Shoulder Pads.

5. Tendon Protectors. These usually are attached to the back of the skates. If they aren't, then buy them. They prevent sharp skates from cutting into the achilles tendon and causing serious and perhaps permanent injury.

Tendon protectors

6. Hip and Thigh Pads. These usually are built into hockey pants; if they aren't, then buy them too.

7. Ankle Guards. These also are a must for defensemen. They are hard, circular protectors defensemen strap around their ankles, and they are a very important part of a defenseman's equipment. Indeed, every defenseman in hockey gets hit at least once a game on the ankle. Ankle guards prevent broken ankles.

8. Cup Protector. Coaches should never permit a player to leave the dressing room—even for a practice skate—without wearing his cup protector.

9. Helmets. Until recently, hockey players were considered cowardly if they wore helmets. Now, after a dozen instances of serious head injuries, resulting mostly from uncontrolled falls, there is a wide movement toward the wearing of helmets. Again, helmets are a must for the young, developing players. If Stan Mikita of the Chicago Black Hawks can wear a helmet, then a ten-year-old Midget Leaguer can too.

Hockey players, by occupation, are not cowards. They don't have to defend their wearing a helmet or an ankle guard or anything else. Indeed, these protectors may save their lives—for a puck traveling 100 miles an hour can inflict severe damage.

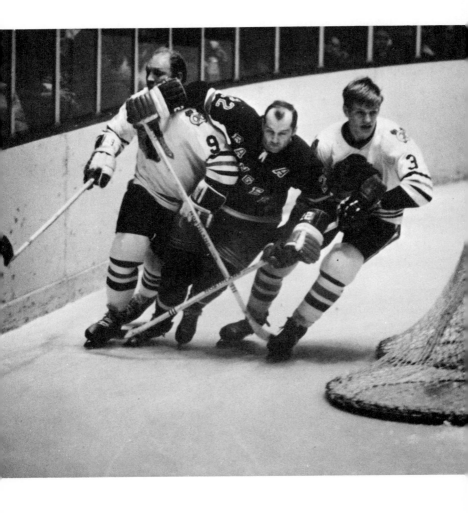

2
Skates and Skating

ALL HOCKEY players must naturally be good skaters: it's impossible to play ice hockey if you cannot skate. Unfortunately, too many developing hockey players don't work hard enough to perfect their skating. Instead, they develop a hard shot or great stickhandling ability or perhaps outstanding defensive qualities. These talents cannot, however, be put to any use at all if the player himself can't skate. It's almost like being a quarterback who can't pass a football.

THE SKATES

Most parents take their nine-year-old son to the local athletic store and, although the boy may have a size-5 foot, buy him a size-9 pair of skates. They tell themselves the boy will grow into the skates within a few years—a rationalization that may be sound, but only economically; there is no way a young boy can skate if his skates are too big. In fact, parents should buy cheaper skates that fit their boy rather than expensive skates that are four sizes too big for him.

Before purchasing his skates, the parents should check to make certain that the skates have a solid toe, firm padding around the ankle area, reinforced inner soles and a dependable blade. Also, the skates should have a tendon protector extending from the back of the heel and protecting the tendon area.

When a player does get a new pair of skates, he must break them in properly; he can't take a new pair of skates out of the box, lace them on, then go onto the ice and skate for 2 hours. If he does, his feet will be sore for a month. There's a definite technique involved in breaking in new skates.

When he laces the new skates, the player must lace them very loosely. Next, he should soak them in a tub of water for several minutes; this helps loosen the leather and forms it to the contours of the player's feet. Then he should go out and skate for 5 or 10 minutes. After that, he should repeat the entire process—soaking and then skating—at least one more time.

Finally, he should take off his wet skates, wipe off the blades and then hang them up for 24 hours in a cool area. (Don't hang them near a radiator or a heater.) The next day the new skates will be form-fitting.

Skate-sharpening is often overdone: many players think they must sharpen their blades twice a day, but the edge on the blade of a skate can hold for two or three days, even with constant use. You can tell if the edge is still on the blade of a skate by running the tip of your thumb gently down the edge of the blade. If the blade is still sharp, it will nearly slice your finger. Another way to tell if your blades are sharp is to stop suddenly on the ice; if your skates fly from under you, then the blade edge is dull.

HOW TO SKATE

Basic form in skating, like basic form in most sports, is mostly the result of an individual's abilities. There are, for instance, trackmen who run erect and there are trackmen who run crouched. There are golfers with long backswings and others with short backswings. Form is mostly personal, and this applies to skating too.

However, the best skaters—the most graceful, the most powerful, and the most agile skaters—all seem to skate the same way. They skate with their knees bent just slightly, their weight always moving forward. They generate power with strong hip action, keep their skates close to the ice, moving with long, smooth strides that look effortless. And they maintain perfect balance at all times, keeping their legs spread well apart.

Hockey players also must be able to skate backward almost as well as they do forward. They must be able to change direction—backward to forward, forward to sideways, sideways to backward—in an instant. If a hockey player can't execute all these maneuvers with great precision, then he really isn't a hockey player.

SKATING DRILLS

The first—and perhaps the longest—part of any hockey practice should be devoted to skating drills. There's no more important part of the game, so it's only reasonable that skating receive more attention than anything else. The best teams always seem to have the best skaters as well as a coach who stresses skating more than anything else. There are a number of excellent skating drills, all designed to improve a player's skating ability and build up his stamina to the point where he can play 2 solid minutes every shift. Stamina is developed only by skating and skating and more skating.

These drills should be a part of every hockey player's practice session, either under a coach's supervision or by himself.

1. Hip Drill. To develop solid hip motion, a skater

skates as fast and as long as he can without lifting his skates off the ice. He must, in fact, work his hips furiously in order to move at all. Cheating at this drill cheats only oneself.

2. Stops and Starts. National Hockey League players look for excuses ("Coach, I've got an injured finger") when the whistle sounds for Stops and Starts. This savage drill should be done backward as well as forward. There are three ways to work this exercise:

> A. A group of players line up at the boards. At the coach's whistle, all skate as fast as they can to the other boards, stop abruptly, turn around and then skate as fast as they can back to the starting position.
>
> B. At the whistle, a line of players at the goal starts skating as fast as they can up ice. The coach blows his whistle whenever he wants them to stop—at the first blue line, the red line, the second blue line, or even the goal line at the far end. Then they turn abruptly and return at full speed to the starting position.
>
> C. A group of players line up at the blue line. At the whistle, they start skating as fast as they can—stopping either at the red line or the other blue line. Then they turn and return at full speed to the starting position.

Practice each of these drills 12 or (if possible) 15 times every day. They help develop stamina and also perfect the ability to stop in an instant and turn back without having to make a wide swing.

3. Agility Drills. The coach lines up three players. At the first whistle they skate away. At the second whistle they turn right. At the third whistle they turn left. At the fourth whistle they skate backward. And so on. Another way to conduct agility drills is to set up a slalom type of obstacle course and have the players skate the course as fast as possible, against a clock. The worst performers should skate the course until their time is satisfactory.

4. Figure 8's. The team starts skating at the faceoff circle at center ice. The players skate as fast as they can around the net, back through center ice and down behind the other net. It is important that they develop the proper crossover technique behind the net, and the Figure 8 is the perfect drill for that. In other words, when a player is skating behind the net, he must be building speed at the same time. He must keep the weight of his body on his inside foot. A player cannot simply glide around the net. If he does, he will end up out near the boards in the corner and find that play has left him behind.

3

The Hockey Stick

A HOCKEY stick is the hockey player's tool: a hockey player without a stick is like a golfer without a golf club.

SELECTING THE PROPER STICK

Hockey players must fit themselves with the proper stick. Goaltenders, of course, have a special stick, discussed in the goaltending chapter. Other players' sticks come in different sizes, weights and shapes. The individual player must settle on a stick that provides him with the best possible feel.

Hockey sticks are made either "left," "right" or "neutral." A left wing, for instance, would use a left stick, since that stick is made for left-handed shooting: that is, the blade is angled so that when a left-handed shooter has the puck on his forehand, he can handle it better. Right wings use right sticks; many centers use neutral sticks—the blade on a neutral stick is not angled; and the center can maneuver the puck on his backhand and his forehand with equal ease.

Sticks come in different lengths, since no player can possibly control either an oversized or undersized stick. To determine the correct length for your stick, stand barefoot with the stick in your hand, holding it so it rests on the point of its toe. The top of the stick should reach your chin —no higher, no lower. Or, if you are wearing skates, the top of your stick should be 3 inches below your chin.

Correct length of the hockey stick, if you are wearing skates.

Sticks also have different lies; that is, they have different angles between the blade and the handle. Most players use between a four- and a seven-lie stick. The four-lie enables the player to carry the puck a great distance away from his skates. A seven-lie stick has a smaller blade-to-handle angle, and is thus more upright, causing the player to carry the puck closer to his skates.

There is no one correct way to select a proper stick lie. A tall player who skates erect should obviously use a number seven-lie stick; a short, squat player who skates with a crouched style should use a number-four stick. The majority of players, though, use a five or a six stick.

Incidentally, you cannot test a stick for the proper lie in your bare feet—the way you test the stick for length. After all, you play hockey with skates—and skates make you taller. So, test sticks for the proper lie when you are on skates.

PRIMING THE HOCKEY STICK

Hockey players in the NHL treat their hockey sticks with great respect, almost the way a golfer treats a putter that just won him the National Open. Most players shave the heel of their stick, and perhaps the toe. This seems to be a psychological quirk: they think it helps them score goals—and perhaps it does.

When a player gets a new stick, the first thing he should do is put a knob on the end of it: either wrap a roll of tape around the end, or attach one of the rubberized knobs available in most athletic stores. The knob is important: players oftentimes will lose control of the stick for a second, and it will start to slide from their hand. If the stick has a knob at the end, they will be able to control it before it gets away. After putting a knob on the handle, the player tapes the blade of the stick, wrapping a thin layer around the center of the blade.

HOLDING THE HOCKEY STICK

Certain aspects of hockey coincide with elements of the game of golf. Holding the hockey stick is one of them. As Rod Gilbert, the high-scoring right wing for the New York Rangers, says, "You should hold the hockey stick just the way you hold a golf club. Hold it in your fingers—not your palm. By holding it in your fingers, you get the maximum wrist action into your shot. Here. Try holding the stick in your palm. Now roll your wrists. See. You do not get any whip action at all. Holding the stick in your fingers gives you plenty of whip."

Players should always hold their stick with both hands. Right-handed people almost always place their right hand at the top of the stick (they are called left shots); left-handers usually place their left hand at the top of the stick (and they, in turn, are called right shots). The position of the lower hand varies according to the situation.

For instance, if the player is stickhandling with the puck, he should keep his hands fairly close together at the top of the stick. This provides him with maximum feel for the puck at the end of his stick.

If the player with the puck wants to make a pass, he should have his bottom hand a bit lower on the stick: he wants to have enough feel and enough power with his lower hand to make a sharp, accurate pass.

Now, if the player with the puck wants to shoot, he moves his lower hand as far down the handle of the stick as possible. The lower he moves his bottom hand, the more force he will get behind his shot.

STICKHANDLING

When the player has the puck on his stick, the opposition naturally wants to take it away from him. The best way to thwart these attempts is to stickhandle away—keep the puck moving with deft motions of the stick, while always working to set up a goal-scoring opportunity.

There is one basic rule of stickhandling: the player must keep his head up and fix his eyes on the situation in front of him. He cannot look down at the puck; if he does, he will find himself knocked down and no longer in possession of the puck. There are two correct ways to control the puck at the end of the stick:

1. Move it from side to side, advancing it slightly with each short, crisp movement. The puck should be controlled with the middle of the blade, which is cupped just a bit so the player can manage the puck with greater ease.

2. Move the puck front to back. The advantage of this type of stickhandling is that it lures the rival defender into a false sense of security: he thinks you are about to lose the puck, and just as he makes his move to take it off your stick, you react quickly and retrieve the puck, sweeping it back and then moving off away from the duped defender.

STICKHANDLING PRACTICE

There are several good drills designed to improve everyone's stickhandling. The first is rather elementary. A player simply takes the puck and skates down the center of the ice, stickhandling side to side all the way, moving head up at top speed, and continuing around the net. As he skates back up ice, head still up and moving at top speed, he moves the puck from front to back, continuing until he skates behind the goal.

In variation of this drill, the coach stations half a dozen players around the ice and orders one player to stickhandle around all of them, varying his stickhandling techniques.

Another stickhandling drill finds the members of a team forming a fairly wide circle. One player takes the puck and skates between and around the players in the circle, all the while looking to his side and behind him to check for teammates who might be in advantageous positions for passes.

Finally, there is the stickhandler's direct confrontation with a goaltender. The puck carrier stickhandles in on the goalie and attempts to fake the goalie out of position. He cannot do this effectively unless his eyes are straight ahead and focused on the goaltender and the goal. The goaltender will always beat a stickhandler if the stickhandler has his

33

eyes down on the puck. This last drill helps teach the stickhandler the importance of keeping his head and eyes up.

PASSING

Hockey is a game played at incredible speed. The movements are hardly planned; they are, in fact, spontaneous. No team enters a hockey game with a "game plan" that tells them the other team is susceptible, say, to passes on the left wing. Indeed, a team may not score identical goals throughout a 78-game schedule, whereas a football team may score three touchdowns a game on a certain pass pattern.

Passing is the key to a good hockey attack. Sharp, crisp passes, perfectly timed, can send a wing in alone on a breakaway, set up an uncovered shooter in front of the goal and, in general, create goals. Teams win hockey games by scoring goals.

The best passing plays are executed by players familiar with the movements of their teammates. Familiarity breeds hockey success. For example, a center who knows that his left wing is likely to cut toward the goal at a certain moment and at a 40-degree angle obviously has a great advantage—particularly if he can make a perfect lead pass to the spot where the wing will be. This is one reason why the best teams in hockey all establish set lines at the start of a season, then keep those lines intact the rest of the year. Teams subject to daily line changes rarely move the puck forward with any precision; in fact, their best scoring plays are invariably off side because of a poorly timed pass.

Passing, like stickhandling and the other subtleties of hockey, is an art. The pass, first of all, must be made while the passer moves in full skating stride. The pass must always lead the receiver. It must never arrive behind the skater or in his skates. The pass also should reach the receiver on the ice; the puck doesn't have to travel all the way along the ice, but it must be on the ice in a relatively flat position when it reaches the receiver.

MAKING A PASS

Basically, there are three types of passes. Before making any of them, the player must be certain that the receiver is not completely covered by a defender. If he is, and the player still makes the pass, the result may be disastrous.

1. *Forehand Pass:* the most frequently used pass in a hockey game. The passer keeps his stick moving in a very low trajectory to the ice, barely raising the blade, and he practically slides the puck to his teammate. (A backhand pass is executed the same way, only the passer makes the motions with his backhand.) The passer must be careful to keep his blade close to the ice; if he raises the blade as he passes, the puck will rise into the air and ruin the pass.

2. *Drop Pass:* an offensive maneuver against which the defensive team is usually powerless. Imagine this: three attackers are skating down against one or two defenders. The puck carrier, stickhandling ahead of one of his teammates, skates right at a defender, then drops the puck and continues straight ahead. His following teammate has an ideal shooting opportunity. When making a drop pass, the player must make certain that he leaves the puck almost dead; that is, he does not want to leave the puck rolling or bounding. To do this, he simply executes a front-to-back stickhandle. When the puck gets to the front, he removes his stick and continues forward. The puck will lie dead.

3. *Flip Pass:* effective when there's a defensive player between the passer and the receiver. Rather than risk a pass along the ice that might be intercepted by the defender, the passer flips the puck up off the toe of his stick toward his teammate. The puck should hit the ice a few feet be-

fore it reaches the receiver, from which point the properly executed flip pass will slide along the ice. Flip passes must be made with the toe of the blade; if they are attempted with the heel, the puck will fly through the air and carry past the receiver. It's almost impossible to control a pass made with the heel of the stick.

Certain passes should never be attempted. The worst possible pass a player can make is the "slap" pass, where the player winds up and slaps the puck in the direction of a teammate. Since a slap pass cannot be controlled, it's a good pass to forget.

Also, a player should never attempt a pass across the front of his own net, or when he cannot see his receiver.

TAKING A PASS

Skating at top speed, the potential receiver has a tough job. He must accept the pass without breaking his stride and, at the same time, must also be aware of the situation in front of him. He must accept the pass cleanly, without a second look at the puck on his stick: second looks are all defensemen need to send puck receivers crashing into the boards. Bob Nevin of the New York Rangers says that puck receivers should work this way:

"They should not hold their stick too taut. If they do, the force of the puck against the stick will send the puck bouncing away. They should hold their stick fairly loosely. Then they should lay the stick over on top of the puck— cupping it. This enables them to control the puck instantly. Also, the player always should try to take a pass on his forehand. One more thing: a receiver must always keep the blade of his stick firmly against the ice. Otherwise the puck will slide away from him."

PASSING DRILLS

Passing drills are relatively simple. Two or three players skate the length of the ice, making rink-wide passes or shorter, very crisp passes between the center and the wing. Or a defenseman may stand beside the goal, making on-the-ice forehand passes to an onrushing attacker who must then receive the pass and get away a quick shot.

CAUTION

Oftentimes teams become too pass-conscious and attempt to make that extra pass when a shot on the goal is really the proper move. When the issue becomes a question of "Shoot or Pass"—always shoot. After all, a shot might mean an instant goal, so shoot the first time.

4

The Offensive Game: Shooting

IN HOCKEY, the point of the game is scoring goals— as many goals as possible. To score a goal, you must shoot the puck with speed, force, and accuracy. The best shooters combine all three elements; a bad shooter may, for example, have a hard shot but be unable to release it fast enough or control where it's going.

HOW TO SHOOT

Before we discuss shooting, we must go back to sticks again. Recently there has been a move to the so-called curved stick for shooters. The blade of the shooter's stick can be curved as much as a half inch from heel to toe, providing him with a more powerful shooting weapon.

Developing players should not use curved sticks. They should use the regular blades and learn how to play hockey with them. Once they are proficient with the straight blade, they can experiment with the curved stick. Also, the curved stick has its drawbacks: for instance, it may help a player shoot a harder forehand that might move unpredictably in mid-air like a knuckle ball; but the curved stick eliminates the backhand shot from the player's shooting arsenal.

Most defensemen do not and should not use curved sticks at all; curved sticks restrict their puck-handling abilities and can lead to goals—for the opposition.

Shooting requires perfect balance, timing and coordination. The shooter fires off his lead foot—the left foot for a right-hand shot, the right foot for a left-hand shot. This places all his power in the proper position. His lower hand is as far down along the handle of the stick as possible. The upper hand steers the stick and the shot; the lower

When you shoot, keep the stick low to the ice.

provides the power. The position of the puck against the blade depends upon the particular type of shot the player wants to make, but the puck must always rest flat on the surface.

After the shot is away, the blade of the stick must follow the puck at the target. (Again this is like golf, where the player follows through after the hit and keeps his club moving toward the cup.)

The height of the shot is the result of the blade angle at impact. If the blade comes down on the puck itself with a closed face, the puck will either skid along the ice or move with a very low trajectory. If the blade hits the puck with an open face, the puck will fly immediately into the air and continue to move along with a high trajectory. Needless to say, the best shots are low, for low shots stay in the rink.

After you shoot, follow through—as in golf—
by forcing the blade out at your target.

THE SHOTS

There are three basic shots all hockey players must learn to execute—or their opportunities to score goals won't mean much.

1. Forehand Wrist Shot. This is the best shot for any hockey player. He can make this shot under most circumstances—and it is the most accurate shot in hockey. The wrists work together: a right-handed shooter's left wrist snaps the stick back; the bottom wrist works against this and snaps the stick forward. A southpaw's shot, of course, simply switches hands. The puck should be as close to the heel of the blade as possible in order to generate more power. Again, the height of a wrist shot is controlled by the angle of the blade as it comes down into the puck.

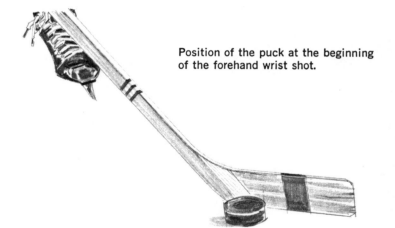

Position of the puck at the beginning of the forehand wrist shot.

2. Backhand Shot. This shot is used mostly by center icemen. Its force is not great, but backhanders usually surprise goaltenders and have a very high scoring ratio. The backhand shot is almost a sweep shot. The player starts

42

the puck in motion well behind his body and then whips the shot at the target. Again, you cannot attempt a backhand shot with a curved blade, because the puck will slide off the stick.

3. Slap Shot. This shot brings the "oohs" and the "aahs" from the spectators, but it has a very low scoring ratio—well below that of a forehand shot. The slap shot comes off the forehand: the player sets himself with both his feet pointing in the general direction of the puck. Barely taking aim, he draws his stick back and then brings it down into the puck—hitting behind the puck and then continuing into the puck. The shot will zoom away in some direction—usually one other than the goal. If you want to be a crowd pleaser, then you should practice the slap shot. However, if you want to be a coach pleaser, then you should spend most of your practice time working on the forehand.

Position of the puck at the beginning of the flip shot.

Two other shots frequently used during a game are the flip shot and the lob shot. The flip shot is made with a little flick of the wrists and with the puck resting against the toe of the blade. It is a soft shot most effective when a player has the goaltender down and must get the puck over him. The lob shot is just that: an arching flip high into the air, shot from considerable distance. The shooter hopes that it will take a fluke bounce when it lands and bounce past the goaltender. This works a few times each season.

Finally, there is one important thing to remember when attempting any of these shots: keep your stick as close to the ice as possible throughout the shooting process. For example, slap shooters who wind up, taking the stick back to shoulder level or higher, sometimes have no puck to hit when they return to the ice. A defensive player will have taken it away.

WHERE TO SHOOT

There's no certain way to score a goal. The best shot each time depends upon the particular angle from which the shooter and the puck are approaching the goal. In the ideal situation, the puck is 15 feet directly in front of the goaltender. From here the best shots a player can take are: (a) low to the corners, either along the ice or 6 inches off it; (b) high to the corners, particularly the stick-side corner; or (c) anywhere just inside the posts.

THE SHOOTING ANGLE

When about to shoot, the player must be aware of one thing: the angle at which his eyes see the goal is not the same angle the puck has on the goal. For instance, a player skating almost head-on at the goaltender and carrying the puck along his right side may see a wide opening to the goalie's right side. But the puck itself doesn't approach the net along the shooter's line of sight; so, sight the target from the position of the puck.

Shooting angle is also discussed from the goaltender's viewpoint on page 78.

DEFLECTING SHOTS

Deflections are the toughest shots for a goaltender to stop. The puck is flying at him in one direction, then an attacking player deflects the puck with his stick, alters its direction and—Red Light—a goal. Deflecting shots is an art: Phil Esposito of the Boston Bruins spends hours every year practicing deflections.

To deflect a puck, simply hold the blade of your stick in its path—aiming the blade in the direction of the goal. If the puck hits your stick, it is likely to deflect toward the goal, but the odds of success increase greatly with practice, until the stick blade can be positioned automatically.

SCREENING SHOTS

Attacking players should always attempt to screen the goaltender's vision; that is, they should position themselves near the net between the goaltender and the play in front of him. This is quite legal, although goalies dislike it and are likely to hit the screening player around the ankles with their sticks. A goalie can't stop what he can't see, and perhaps one third of all goals scored in hockey result from screened shots.

PRACTICE SHOOTING

The best players practice their shooting all year long. To start, they develop their wrists—squeezing rubber balls, working with weights, rolling bars, and so forth. They also devise their own shooting targets in backyards or anyplace else they can work at the game. Shooting targets are easy to make: simply mark off the dimensions of a net—6 feet wide, 4 feet high—against a garage or a board; then find a smooth shooting surface—not cement or dirt or grass, but something very glossy, like linoleum. Practice for at least an hour each day. Pick out a spot and try to fire ten successive shots at it without missing. Move out, move in, move to the side. Develop your shot to the point where you can fire the puck exactly where you want it.

There are a number of excellent on-ice shooting drills. At the start of a practice, the players all line up at the blue line. Then, each player in turn takes the puck and moves in for a shot—any shot he prefers. Later, a defenseman should position himself to the side of the goal and pass the puck to the oncoming shooter, who must receive the pass and shoot with great haste and great accuracy. There are also the various two-on-one and three-on-two attacks, all designed to enable an attacking player to get off a shot on the goal.

5
The Offensive Game: Attacking

BEFORE a team can attempt to score a goal, it must establish an organized pattern for its attack. This demands total teamwork by all players; there's no place for individuals in hockey.

The first, and perhaps the most important, part of hockey teamwork is the composition of forward lines. The ideal forward line consists of a center who can make plays and score goals, one wing who excels in scoring and another wing who is strong on defense.

The best lines in the NHL are made up that way. The Boston Bruins' line of center Phil Esposito and wings Ken Hodge and Wayne Cashman set a league scoring record for a forward line in 1970–71. Esposito scored 76 goals and had an incredible 76 assists. He was the ultimate center. Hodge, the right wing, scored 43 goals. Cashman, the left wing, scored only 21 goals but was a superb defensive wing—and an ideal man for getting the puck to Esposito and Hodge from the corners.

Basically, the center's job is maneuvering the puck to set up scoring chances, either by setting up his wings with crisp feeding passes or making his own scoring opportunities. Wings should skate their lanes and not go roaming about the ice. The right wing, for example, should never cross onto the left side of the ice on the attack. Instead, both wings should remain in their lanes, waiting for the center to make a move with the puck.

When the puck enters the attacking zone, the wings must still play a bit cautiously. One of them should always remain in position to head back in the other direction in case the defensive team captures the puck and starts its own rush. If the puck is in the right side of the attacking zone, then the right wing pursues it, and the left wing trails in his lane. If the puck is in the left zone, then the left wing follows it, while the right wing remains back on his side. The center should float around the attacking zone, staying within shooting range of the goal.

The role of the defensemen on the attack has changed in recent years. Until the late 1950's, defensemen were just that. When they stopped the rival team's rushes, they left the puck for a forward to carry away, or they perhaps made a short, harmless pass. Nowadays defensemen are more offensive-minded. Still, defensemen should not primarily be puck carriers. Occasionally they can make a rush up the ice, but their basic job is defense—and they shouldn't forget it. When they reach the blue line in the attacking zone, defensemen must play cautiously. They cannot risk a move deeper into the attacking zone because the opposition will then have a manpower advantage if it can get the puck onto the attack and out of the zone. Defensemen should develop low, hard shots and should also perfect their ability to make crisp, direct passes. Bad passes by defensemen usually mean goals for the other team.

THE PLAYS

Despite hockey's incredible speed, there are a number of prepared, offensive plays that all teams should practice.

1. Headmanning. This is a tactic favored by the Montreal Canadiens. Headmanning simply means getting the puck to the lead skater in the attack. For example, the puck carrier skating around the red line spots a teammate breaking down the left wing. He must make his pass instantly—hitting the wing before he skates off side.

2. The Center Rush. Most teams prefer to have the center skate the puck into the attacking zone and then generate a scoring play. The most important thing for the center to do is get across the blue line fast. Too many centers hesitate and swerve before they cross the blue line, consequently taking their wings off side.

3. Breakaways. A breakaway is the prettiest play in hockey. The skater simply moves in alone on the goaltender. However, breakaway goals are not so easy to score as one might imagine. The puck carrier just has too much time to think about how to beat the goalie, and oftentimes he outsmarts himself and never even gets off a decent shot. On a breakaway, if the attacker is approaching the goalie head-on, he should shoot for the corner—either corner—from about 15 feet out. If he approaches from the wing, he has two alternatives, provided he cradles the puck on the stick along his side and not in front of him. He can (a) shoot on the goal or (b) fake a shot, pull the puck in front of the goaltender and then slide it into the net. Players shouldn't attempt to fake the goalie head-on, because they will then have only about one third of the net to shoot into by the time they've completed their fake and moved to one side.

49

4. Power Plays. A team receives a big lift if it can score consistently on the power play, which occurs any time a team has a player advantage on the ice due to a penalty to the opposition. The object is to move the puck cautiously forward, isolate one player near the goal, then hit him with a pass and hope he can score. There is no great rush; indeed, the attacking team should wait to set up a player with the best shot. Organization is the key to an effective power play, and a team should have an out-

Headmanning the puck is the fastest way to get into the attacking zone. The puck carrier must be alert and make a crisp pass to the lead skater —the head man—on the attacking team.

standing shooter and puck handler working at one point on the blue line, with a good offensive defenseman working the other point. A coach should attempt to use a regular forward line during a power play; but if a team has a player particularly adept at tip-ins and deflections, he should play one of the wings.

The center has three basic options on a three-on-two rush. All require proper execution and, more importantly, familiarity with your line mates.

5. Three-on-Two. This is the basic rush in a hockey game. Three forwards—one line—break in on two defensemen. The center should carry the puck, so he can dictate the play. He has a number of alternatives:

A. He can continue through the center of the ice, slowing down and waiting for his wings to break toward the goal. Then he can either shoot for the goal, knowing that his wings will be in good position to collect a possible rebound, or slip a pass to one of the wings.

B. He can swerve to one side after crossing the blue line, at the same time knowing the far wing will go for the goal. Then he can pass to the wing near the goal mouth.

C. He can set up for a drop-pass situation. He simply carries straight in on the goal, signaling a wing to skate behind him. Then he leaves the puck for the trailing wing, who will have a clear shot at the goal.

Centers familiar with their wingmen can improvise plays quite easily, developing from these three.

If a wingman carries the puck into the attacking zone, he should continue to skate forward with one of three moves in mind: (a) angling toward the goal and trying to hit the opposite wing with a goal mouth pass; (b) angling toward the goal and then shooting himself; or (c) sliding a back pass to the trailing center, who must be skating near the middle of the ice, head-on toward the goal.

6. Two-on-One. The puck carrier should attempt to shoot the puck on goal when he has a two-on-one situation. Too many players attempt a pass to their teammate, and it will usually backfire. The puck carrier shouldn't tip his move, though: if he plans to shoot, he should fake the pass first. If he wants to pass, he should fake the shot first.

Drawing the puck on the backhand
to a teammate in a shooting position
is the best offensive maneuver on a
faceoff.

7. Faceoffs. Good centers can initiate scoring plays
right from faceoffs. To start, the players must position
themselves correctly: if the faceoff is to the goalie's left,
then the right wing should station himself behind and to
the left of the center. If the faceoff is to the goalie's right,

then the left wing should station himself behind and to the right of the center. On the faceoff, the center usually attempts to draw the puck to the wing or a defenseman, who then will have a clear shot on the goal. The centers can vary their faceoff tactics. They can shoot the puck off

Shooting the puck on the faceoff is a chancy proposition: if it works, fine—but most of the time it doesn't, and the defensive team takes control.

the faceoff themselves; they can slap it into the corner and attempt to gain control there. Faceoff goals discourage rival teams.

REMINDER

Shoot when you have an open shot. Avoid the extra pass. Never pass to a covered teammate.

6
The Defensive Game

THE STARTING lineup for a hockey team lists six players —a center iceman, a left wing, a right wing, a left defenseman, a right defenseman and a goaltender. Despite the various names for their positions, all six players are actually defensemen: each player has a specific defensive assignment at all times.

Eddie Giacomin, the goaltender for the New York Rangers, says, "The goalie makes the final mistake by giving up the goal. But at least one other player on his team made an earlier mistake that set up the goal-scoring opportunity."

The best hockey players are "two-way"; that is, they not only score goals but they also skate back on defense to help prevent the opposition from scoring.

Indeed, one of the best indicators for determining the value of a forward (a center or a left wing or a right wing) is the "plus and minus" system used by all teams in the NHL. The system works two ways:

1. Say a left wing scores a goal for the opposition. Well,

the player charged with defending against the left wing is the right wing. So the right wing receives a minus-one for permitting his rival to score. Then when the right wing himself scores a goal, he receives a plus-one. A player with a bad minus record at the end of a season oftentimes finds himself wearing a different uniform the next year.

2. When a team scores a goal, each player on the ice at the time of the goal receives a plus-one. However, when a team is scored upon, each player on the ice receives a minus-one. Members of forward lines with poor defensive records generally have little bargaining power at contract time.

THE ART OF CHECKING

Checking is the most important aspect of defensive play. Checking can be accomplished with either deft movements of a stick or violent, vicious motions of a body. Checking is the essence of defense. Here are the forms of checking all developing hockey players must learn:

1. Fore Checking. This is an involved act requiring the efforts of all three forwards. The object of fore checking is to pin the opposition team deep in its own end and close down the normal lanes into the attacking zone. The center initiates the fore checking by trying to harass the puck carrier. If the puck carrier then tries to skate to his right in order to avoid the fore-checking center, the left wing, in turn, moves in against him and almost double-teams him. If the puck carrier tries to skate out to his left, then the right wing must skate in and attempt to force him back. This harassment should confuse the puck carrier to the extent that he will make a bad clearing pass or, even better, lose the puck to one of the fore checkers.

Only two forwards—the center and either of his wings—can fore-check at the same time. If the right wing moves in to help the center, then the left wing must remain back at least 30 feet, ready to skate away in the event the opposition team does break away from the fore checkers and starts a rush up ice. If all three forwards get themselves caught checking too deeply, the result is usually disaster.

Bob Nevin of the New York Rangers, one of the best defensive forwards in the NHL, says the trick to fore checking is relatively simple: "Never face the puck carrier head-on when you fore-check. Approach him at an angle. Then he must maneuver in some direction, and you have a better chance to detach him from the puck. Also, when you fore-check, play the man—not the puck. If you can eliminate the puck carrier, then the player fore-checking with you should be able to pick up the loose puck and start a good scoring effort himself."

2. Back Checking. Oftentimes teams cannot get into position to initiate a fore-checking type of defense. When this happens, the forwards must then resort to back checking. Simply explained, back checking finds a forward skating side by side with an attacking player, ready to intercept a pass or make any other defensive play that might prevent a goal.

Back checkers must always remain alert. They must never skate ahead of their rival forwards; if they do, the rivals can cut behind them and slip into position to accept a pass. Back checkers must try to keep their rival between themselves and the boards, then force the opponent into the boards and out of the play.

3. Poke Checking. When a defender is confronted with a one-on-one situation, one of his best defensive weapons is the poke check. The defender, who is facing the puck carrier, makes a one-handed poke at the puck with his stick. If he misses the puck, he will probably hit the puck carrier's stick. A well-executed poke check will disrupt the puck carrier's maneuvering and leave him without a puck to carry.

Here, the two defensemen converge upon an offensive player, and with body checks—one high, one low—break up the play. Properly executed, this is an effective defensive move.

4. Body Checking. This is the glamorous part of defensive play. Spectators appreciate body checking more than any other type of checking. However, body checking should be attempted only when the situation is "right"; that is, when the body checker himself is not the final man remaining in the line of defense protecting the goaltender.

Body checking requires perfect timing. When a puck carrier is skating with his head down, that's the perfect time to hit him with a crunching body check. When a rival is preoccupied with the pass he's just taken from a teammate, that's the perfect time to smack him onto the ice.

The best body checkers establish themselves early in a game. They cruise around and body check the first rival they meet and try to destroy him. If they don't destroy the player, they have at least intimidated him. Hopefully, they will also intimidate his teammates. And usually they do: most of the time the recipient of that first check will skate around harmlessly the rest of the game, not wanting to expose himself to another vicious body check, and his teammates find themselves avoiding body contact at all costs. A team intimidated is a team defeated. The Boston Bruins used this approach in the late 1960's with great success.

There are, of course, necessary limits in the jungle of body checking. Body checkers cannot take more than two steps at a rival before they hit him. If they do, they receive a penalty for charging. They cannot elbow-check, leg-check, and so on. Body checking must be done very cleanly.

The best body checkers never watch the puck or the stick or the eyes or the legs of their intended victim. Instead, they look directly at his chest. There are no "chest fakes" in hockey. Then they maneuver themselves so that their own body is in direct line with the victim's chest. Next comes the check.

The checker must take a wide stance, with one foot behind the other. He pushes off that rear foot and smacks the puck carrier with his shoulder—digging it into the other player's chest. This is the best type of body check and the most effective.

5. Hip Checking. This is another effective form of checking, and it too is a glamorous check, because the recipient often does a somersault and loses his stick or gloves in mid-air. It is a particularly good check for forwards to use in the neutral zone. The hip check also is one of the defensemen's best weapons, particularly when a puck carrier skates along the boards.

This is how to give a good hip check: crouch and then skate sideways or backward into the puck carrier's line of flight. If you simply touch the puck carrier with your hip, he will fly into the air and the puck will roll harmlessly away. If you make direct contact, he will do a neat sag. No matter how lightly you hit the puck carrier with a hip check, he will lose control of the puck.

REMINDER

Never attempt a body check when you are the only player defending a two-on-one attack or, for that matter, whenever you are outnumbered.

Also, when you decide to make a body, hip, or any other check, make certain that you complete it. Never let the intended victim get past you. If he does, the result will probably be a goal.

MORE TRICKS

One of the prettiest plays in hockey is the so-called stick lift. The stick lift is executed by a defensive player, and when it is done well, the defender makes the puck carrier feel like a two-year-old boy back on a pond. Stick lifting is not difficult. A back-checking player, skating close to his rival, simply lifts his rival's stick from the ice by hooking it at the heel with his own stick. The stick lift, properly executed, can stop pass plays and shot attempts. And that, after all, is the job of the back checker.

Finally, there is the sweep check, which is a version of the aforementioned poke check. However, instead of thrusting his stick at the puck and the stick of the puck carrier, the defensive player sweeps his stick at both the puck and

The stick lift.

the stick of the puck carrier. This is not so sophisticated a maneuver as the poke check, but it can be just as effective.

PLUSES

Defensive-style players are an asset on any hockey team. Keep your own plus and minus record as evidence of your defensive ability—or inability. If defense is your weak point, then you're a bad hockey player.

7

Playing Defense

DEFENSEMEN are not expected to be two-way players. Their primary concern is to defend their goaltender against opposition attack. They must attempt to keep the puck as far away from their goal as possible. If a defenseman can do that job well, he is a valuable performer for a team. If the same defenseman can also skate the puck out of his own zone and set up goal-scoring opportunities for his team at the other end of the ice, then he is a super player.

There is one super defenseman in hockey today. He is Bobby Orr, the young star of the Boston Bruins. As a rookie in 1966–67, Orr was voted the Rookie Of The Year and was also elected to the League's all-star second team. In 1967–68, 68–69, 69–70, and 70–71, he was voted the League's best defenseman and was elected to the all-star first team. Orr has also established records for defensemen by scoring 37 goals in a season and accumulating a total of 139 points in a single year—unheard-of statistics before Orr's arrival.

However, defensemen who can play like Bobby Orr are

rare. Although developing young defensemen can idolize an Orr and attempt to copy his movements on the ice, they cannot expect to be good defensemen unless they have a solid background and understanding of the basics of their position.

THE BASICS OF DEFENSE

1. All defensemen must be able to skate backward at least as well as they do forward. While moving in reverse, defensemen must also be ready to turn away in another direction if the puck carrier makes a motion to elude them. While skating backward, defensemen should always be moving slightly into the path of the oncoming opponent. This forces the opponent into a more difficult shooting or passing position. When a defenseman stops moving in reverse and wants to start forward again, he must head off with very short, choppy skating strides. This will help him build momentum quickly. Defensemen must practice skating backward whenever they can.

2. Defensemen must learn to get the puck out of their defensive zone as quickly as possible. When a defenseman disrupts an opposition attack, he should control the puck and make an immediate positive play to get the puck into the neutral zone, where it will be harmless for a few moments. The best defensemen learn how to make perfect passes to their attacking teammates. No matter what, the defenseman must clear the puck instantly. If he doesn't, the result is likely to be a goal for the opposition.

3. Defensemen must never control the puck in their own end IF they are the last line of protection in front of their goaltender. One mistake and BOOM—a goal for the other team. Never attempt to stickhandle in your defensive zone unless there's a teammate nearby to take a pass if an emergency develops.

4. Defensemen must never skate in front of their net with the puck. They must also never pass the puck across the front of their net to a teammate on the other side. An efficient fore checker for the other team could often steal the puck and have an excellent goal-scoring opportunity for himself. Always skate behind the net and then pass the puck around it to a teammate on the other side.

5. Defensemen must be proficient poke checkers. A stick is the defenseman's calling card. The slightest poke at a puck can disrupt an attack.

6. One defenseman must always remain in front of his net to protect the goaltender. When the puck is in the corner to the goalie's right, then the right defenseman goes after it and the left defenseman remains in front of the goaltender. If the puck goes into the left corner, then the right defenseman stays in front of the goal. Defensemen should never leave their goaltender naked; when they do, the result is usually disaster.

7. All defensemen must develop strong shots from the so-called point—the blue line. The best shots by a defenseman are either along the ice or very low to the ice. Such shots make for easy deflections and are more difficult for a goaltender to follow in a maze of players. Never shoot high: the goalie catches high shots very easily and can then direct the puck to one of his teammates.

Shots from the point don't have to be pinpointed; that is, a defenseman does not have to aim for the corner. After all, a shot from 60 feet will hardly be accurate. Shoot into a group of players: the goalie may lose sight of the puck, and a teammate may have a good chance to deflect it into the goal.

8. The final basic rule is perhaps the most important. The defenseman should always be between the goalie and the puck carrier or another rival player. When moving on

defense, in other words, never permit the puck carrier or any other rival player to get between you and the goaltender. This is the key to a good defensive effort.

CONFRONTATIONS

Defensemen always find themselves face to face with trouble. For a defenseman, trouble is a rival player either carrying the puck or moving into position to accept a pass near the goal. How a defenseman reacts to trouble generally determines the outcome of a hockey game.

Normally, defensemen prefer to block shots themselves. This is a risky business: a defenseman cannot go down to one knee and attempt to block a shot unless the shooter is within about 5 feet of him. Otherwise, the shot is likely to rise up and hit him in the face. Indeed, defensemen should never go down to block a shot if the shooter is more than a stick-length away. When a defenseman does go down to block a shot, he must drop to one knee only; if he goes down on both knees, he cannot recover fast enough.

Often the situation doesn't permit the defenseman to block a shot himself. Here are the correct ways for a defenseman to react to the various attacks he is likely to see during a game:

1. One-against-One. The defenseman is skating backward, facing the puck carrier. Forget the puck. Think about the carrier: you must eliminate the player from the play. Do not commit yourself. Be aware of eye fakes and leg fakes and stick fakes. Watch the puck carrier's chest and then move against his chest to ride him out of the play. Always stay between the puck carrier and your goaltender. Work to force the puck carrier against the boards. If all else fails, try to force the puck carrier onto his backhand side. A defenseman should not be beaten in a one-on-one situation.

2. Two-on-One. This is a delicate situation for a defenseman. If he moves out to stop the puck carrier, then the carrier, in turn, can send a pass to his now-uncovered teammate, and that player will have a clear shot on the goal. If he moves to protect against a possible pass, then the puck carrier himself can skate right in for a clear shot. There is only one correct way for a defenseman to handle this predicament. Skating backward, the lone defenseman must remain almost between the two attacking players—favoring the puck carrier's side just a bit. This particular tactic helps ward off a pass. At the same time, it forces the puck carrier to a bad shooting angle. The goaltender should be able to handle the bad-angle shot without much difficulty.

3. Two-on-Two. The defensemen, skating backward, should be staggered, the defenseman on the side of the puck carrier skating a stride or two ahead of his defense mate. That lead man must attempt to eliminate the puck carrier—playing the man, not the puck. If the puck carrier eludes the defenseman, then the situation becomes two-on-one—and the remaining defenseman must react as explained above.

4. Three-on-Two. This must be handled much like a two-on-two. The defensemen must stagger themselves, with the man on the side of the puck carrier staying ahead of his defense partner. The lead defenseman must try to force a pass play and also prevent the puck carrier from getting off the first shot. The other defenseman must be ready to react in the direction of the pass, positioning himself so that he can block a shot and also eliminate the threat of a second pass. The lead defenseman must look out for a drop pass, perhaps the best type of maneuver the puck carrier can make under three-on-two circumstances.

5. Three-on-One. There is no real way to handle this predicament. Remain in the middle of the ice and do not back up into your goaltender. The opposition will almost certainly get off a shot, so position yourself to clear the rebound—if there is one.

THE TRICKS OF DEFENSE

Once a developing player has a sound understanding of the basics of defensive play, he can move ahead and learn some of the tricks of his position. Most of these tricks are legal; all of them will make the defenseman's job much easier.

Defensemen are told not to allow rival players to stand around in front of the goaltender, waiting for a pass or a chance to deflect a shot or a rebound. How do defensemen discourage these opponents? There are two easy ways, both guaranteed to reduce traffic congestion near the goal:

1. Pushing, whacking opponents lightly on the ankle, and holding their sticks, while not always legal, can be effective deterrents. And elbowing, though illegal, is also most effective.

2. A player whose stick is not on the ice is relatively harmless, so defensemen can use their sticks to lift other players' sticks off the ice. It's not legal for defensemen to use their sticks like five irons, cracking them against their opponents' sticks, but it's another trick that works.

REMINDER

Defensemen must play defense. They are not on the ice to score goals. They are out there to prevent goals.

When a defenseman steps onto the ice to take his shift, he must have three things in his mind: (a) make certain a defensman is always in front of the goaltender; (b) make certain an attacking player doesn't get between the defenseman and the goaltender; and (c) make certain the puck takes the fastest, safest route out of the defensive zone.

72

8

Goaltending

THE HOCKEY player with the most demanding job is the goaltender, that heavily padded, masked man crouching between the red posts, waiting for the shooters to begin their frenzied assault on his 4-by-6-foot cage.

Goaltenders are lonely men. When the shooters fire the puck 100 miles an hour past them into the net, the goalies, in the eyes of all spectators and the writers in the press box, have been "beaten." All losses are blamed on the goalies; only goaltenders have bad nights in hockey. When a team wins a game, however, it wins because the shooters with the curved sticks scored a few goals—not because its own goaltender has played superbly. Goalies never win hockey games.

EQUIPMENT

Owing to the hazardous nature of his job, a goaltender must wear more and bulkier protective equipment than any other player on the ice. The equipment must also be lightweight enough to permit the goalie free and easy movement during a game.

First of all, he needs goalie skates, which differ from the skates used by regular players: the entire blade on a goalie's skate meets the ice, making it easier for the goalie to stand motionless during stops in the action. A goaltender never gets a bench respite during a game; he is on the ice for the duration. The blades are so constructed that it is impossible for a puck to slip between boot and blade. The latter doesn't have an edge, unlike other skates, so the goalie can slide sideways between the goalposts. The goalie's special skates also have extra protection around the toes and the ankles.

The bulky shin pads must fit comfortably against a goalie's legs. These pads should not be too heavy, though: good goalies prefer to feel the puck when it strikes against their leg pads. They say it keeps them in the game. The goalie's uniform pants have interior pockets for thigh pads, and should be so well padded that there is not one inch of unprotected leg above the top of the shin pads. Goalies, naturally, must wear the best protective cup available.

All goalies wear chest protectors, but there is no need to wear an oversized protector. Pucks rarely strike against a goalie's chest, and when they do, the goalie is usually moving and can easily absorb the force of the shot.

A goaltender must also wear shoulder pads, arm pads, and elbow pads. All this equipment must be heavier and more protective on the goalie's stick side, where there's no glove to catch shots. The back of the stick-hand glove must have almost steel-like protection. About the only way to stop a shot on your stick side is to throw some part of your body at it. Consequently, the possible parts must always be well protected.

The goalie's catching glove is almost like a first baseman's mitt: it has a big, flexible webbing and should feel com-

74

fortable on the goalie's hand. The glove should also have an extra-long sleeve top that reaches almost to the elbow, to prevent pucks from breaking wrists and other bones.

Stick selection is an individual choice. Select a lie that will allow the blade of the stick to rest completely along the ice when you hold the stick in a natural position.

Nowadays the great majority of goaltenders, NHL and Midget League, wear face masks. Until Jacques Plante decided to wear a mask in an NHL game, all goalies who did wear masks were regarded with suspicion. Other players said contemptuously, "The goalie has lost his nerve." When Plante, the greatest goalie of his day, donned a mask, all talk ceased immediately.

All goalies should wear face masks. The puck travels too fast and moves too erratically for any goalie to trust his instincts and reflexes to the point where they're the only protection for his face.

STYLES OF PLAY

There is no such thing as a textbook goaltender. A young, developing goalie should attempt to refine his own style and not try to pattern himself identically after another goaltender.

The best goalies now playing in the NHL all have different styles. Glenn Hall, for instance, is a scrambler who flops all over the ice and challenges the shooters to skate in and beat him. Jacques Plante prefers to roam about, always standing erect, and play the angles—trying, that is, to minimize the size of the net by skating toward the shooter and blocking out portions of the net with his body. Eddie Giacomin plays a combination of the Hall and Plante styles. He flops like Hall, but he also roams about like Plante. The most important thing about all three goalies is that they are among the best puck stoppers in hockey history.

The goalie should always shift his position in front of the net to put himself between the puck and the net. Here, the goalie slides across the crease, keeping his eyes on the puck and being ready for a shot.

There are, however, certain rules that apply to all styles of goaltending:

1. Always watch the puck. Never anticipate its flight or roll. The best goaltenders have learned, much to their embarrassment, that deflections can turn a seemingly harmless shot into an unexpected goal.

2. Play the puck—and the puck handler—at all times. When a skater has the puck on his stick, think primarily about him—not one of his teammates who might be in position for a pass.

3. Set yourself so that your shin pads are centered on the puck. Keep your shin pads hard against each other; never open your legs—or the puck will probably fly through the space between.

4. When you do drop to the ice (all goalies, stand-up types or scramblers, must go down sometimes), get up as

fast as possible. A goalie on the ice means there's a wide expanse of vacant net. The worst shooters can put the puck into an open net.

5. Never roam about the ice to stop pucks unless you know you will get to the puck before a rival player.

6. Keep the puck away from the goal mouth. Direct the puck into the corners with your stick or your skates. If the puck remains around the goal mouth for too long (1 second is really too long), fall on it and get a faceoff.

7. Catch the puck whenever possible. This prevents rebounds and permits you to play the puck in any direction.

8. Keep talking. The best goaltenders are like quarterbacks; they direct the movements of their players in the defensive zone, advising them of the dangers of the situation, keeping them alert with shouts of encouragement.

STOPPING SHOTS

Still, the most difficult part of playing goal is trying to stop the shots. Here is the recommended thinking on the various situations that develop during a hockey game:

1. Playing Long Shots. Never stab at the puck with your glove hand. Get as much body behind the puck as possible. That way, if you miss the puck with your glove, you will stop it with your body. On long, bouncing shots— the type of shot that makes all goalies feel sixty-five years old—play the puck itself: don't let the puck play you. Handle bouncing pucks as fast as possible. If necessary, drop down and smother a bounding puck. Also, approach bouncing pucks head-on, that is, with your stick, glove and body all moving at the puck—ready to give you triple protection against a crazy bounce.

2. Playing the Angles. When a shooter skates down one of the wings at the goaltender, the goalie, in turn, must skate out at the shooter and attempt to reduce his angle on the target. That is, the goalie wants the puck to "see" the least possible amount of open net. Since goalies naturally react faster with their glove hand, they can cheat a bit and expose more goal on their glove side. It is a cardinal sin for the goaltender to be beaten on the so-called short side; that is, the side closest to the puck.

3. Playing Screen Shots. When a shooter fires the puck into a melee of players, the goaltender is helpless. He cannot see the puck, and he doesn't know the direction from which it will come at him. The best goaltenders position themselves directly behind a defenseman and stay on their feet. Screened shots, incidentally, are an excellent advertisement for face masks.

4. Playing the Posts. When the puck is in the corner to the goaltender's left or right, the goalie must position himself so that it is impossible for a shooter to score from beside or behind the net. There are two acceptable ways for a goalie to handle this crisis: (a) he can wrap his outside foot (the foot closest to the puck) around the outside of his goal post; or (b) he can keep the same foot hard

The best way to play the post is to
keep the leg hard against the inside
of the post.

against the inside of the post. Both techniques are effective.
However, the latter permits the goalie to move faster if
the puck is passed around behind him or is centered into
the middle of the ice.

Playing faceoffs.

5. Playing Faceoffs. The goalie must have a clear line of sight to the red faceoff drop area, or else he's beaten at the start. When he sets up, the goalie should position himself at the corner of his crease so the middle of the bottom of his stick rests exactly on the point of his crease.

6. Playing Breakaways. This is mostly a match of wits. The goalie should establish himself immediately. First, he should skate out of his net a few feet, moving at the shooter. This will cut down the shooter's angle and may convince the shooter that he has to fake the goalie. Goaltenders don't want breakaway skaters to shoot; they want them to dribble around and try various fakes. By coming out of his net, the goalie almost eliminates the shot. Then the goalie should try to force the shooter to his own backhand—a difficult type of maneuver. By the time all this has taken place, the goalie has probably confused the shooter so much that the shot itself becomes a routine save.

REMINDERS

All the advice in this chapter will be useless unless the developing goaltender remembers the basics of his position: (a) eyes on the puck at all times; (b) stick on the ice at all times; (c) no loose pucks in front of the net at any time; and (d) goalie in the net at all times.

HOW TO PRACTICE

There are a number of seemingly savage drills that sharpen the movements and reactions of a goaltender. One of the best, and one that frightens spectators at practice sessions, begins with ten or so shooters, each with a puck, lined across the ice about 15 feet in front of the goalie. At the coach's signal a shooter at one end will fire away; then in rapid succession all other shooters fire at the goalie too. This drill can be varied so that the goalie must move from side to side for every shot.

Another drill finds the goalie confronted with a two-man breakaway. The puck carrier shoots; then the trailer attempts to convert the rebound. This drill can also be varied to provide an even tougher challenge for the goalie.

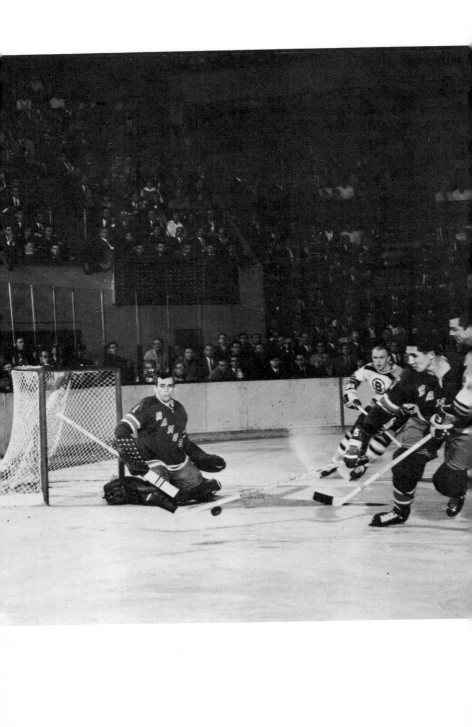

9

Puck Control On Defense

THREE of the most critical maneuvers in hockey are faceoffs, breakout plays designed to get the puck out of the defensive zone and into position for an attack at the opposite end of the ice, and penalty killing. Lost faceoffs can mean lost games; poor breakout plays can mean goals for the opposition; inefficient penalty killers can mean disaster. Unfortunately, most hockey teams don't spend enough time practicing these important maneuvers that generally make the difference between a victory and a defeat.

FACEOFFS

This word is certainly appropriate. Two players, usually the rival centers on the ice at a particular moment, square off face to face, less than a stick's length apart. An official drops the puck between them—and may the best man win.

There is a certain technique involved in faceoff competition. As a center lines up for a faceoff, he must set his skates squarely and rather far apart, with his weight on the balls of his feet. This provides him with sufficient balance and strength to handle the struggle for the puck. He must also keep the blade of his stick flat on the ice and his lower hand well down on the shaft of the stick. A player whose hands are set close together will be overpowered during a faceoff because he'll have no control over the actions of his stick.

The faceoff position: centers with sticks down, weight on the balls of their feet, eyes coordinated between the toe of the stick and the referee's hand.

The best players make detailed studies of faceoffs. They study all the officials: if an official pulls his left skate away the exact moment he releases the puck, a faceoff man should be aware of that habit. If a referee tends to drop the puck very slowly—that is, without any wrist motion—the faceoff man should know that too. Developing faceoff men must study the officials' movements, not only when actually facing off, but also when resting on the bench.

Study the rival faceoff men too. Learn their favorite moves, then find the best counter moves. One of the best faceoff men in hockey today is Derek Sanderson, the slick center of the Boston Bruins. Sanderson wins more than 80 percent of his faceoffs during a season—an incredibly high percentage.

Before stepping into the faceoff area, check your teammates individually to make certain they are ready for the play. Check your wingmen first, then your defensemen, and finally—but most importantly—check your goaltender. Never step into a faceoff area unless your goaltender has signaled you that he is ready for the play. Given the goalie's signal, you can skate in for the faceoff.

The first part of a faceoff is a reflex movement. As the faceoff man settles into position, he must keep his attention largely trained on the spot between the toes of the sticks, where the official will drop the puck. However, he also must somehow peek out the corner of his eye to see when the referee does drop the puck.

WHAT TO DO

The faceoff man must know what he wants to do with the puck before the referee releases it. Basically there are three possible maneuvers on a faceoff and "right" or "wrong" circumstances for each one. The faceoff man can:

1. Whack at the stick of his rival faceoff man, knocking it away from the puck, and then try to control the puck himself.

2. Jab at the puck, thrusting his stick at it, and try to hit it in some advantageous direction—maybe into the boards, maybe down the ice.

3. Draw the puck to a nearby teammate.

FACEOFF ALIGNMENTS

This is one of the two most frequently used alignments for a faceoff in the defensive zone, that is, a faceoff to the goalie's right or to his left. The offensive team here has set up so the left wing is in good shooting position, and the center will try to draw the puck back to him.

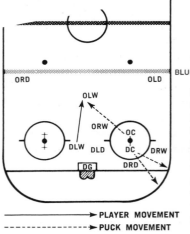

BLUE LINE

On the faceoff, offensive center (OC) wants to set up offensive left wing (OLW); defensive center (DC) wants to get puck back to defensive right wing (DRW) or to defensive right defenseman (DRD). If puck goes from OC to OLW, defensive left wing (DLW) charges at OLW. This plan works in reverse, from the other faceoff circle, with OC trying to set up offensive right wing (ORW).

→ PLAYER MOVEMENT
------→ PUCK MOVEMENT

The best defensive alignment against this tactic places four players up on the faceoff line, with a defenseman remaining back near the goaltender to control the puck if it happens to come in his direction. It is imperative that the defensive center either hit the puck into the right boards, where his right wing will be able to control it. Under no circumstances should the center direct the puck toward the goal itself.

If the defensive center loses the faceoff, the defensive

players must react swiftly. The right wing skates up along the boards to keep the puck from the left defenseman. The center shadows the offensive center, who will skate in front of the net and attempt to deflect a shot or pick up a loose rebound. The left wing covers the opposite side of the ice, checking out the right defensemen. The left defenseman, who set up along the faceoff line, moves out to thwart the left wing. The right defenseman remains near the goal, ready to protect his goaltender.

However, some offensive teams prefer to use this alignment when there is a faceoff in the other team's defensive zone—again, to the goalie's left or to his right. They place all three forwards up on the faceoff line. The faceoff man, the center, will try to draw the puck to one of his defensemen, who, in turn, will pass to his defensive partner. That player might then have a clear shot on the goal.

Here the defensive faceoff man must draw the puck back against the boards and away from his goaltender. There will be a defenseman ready to control the loose puck and initiate an offensive. If the center loses the faceoff, however, the defensive players all have assigned jobs. The right

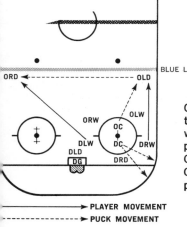

BLUE LINE

On the faceoff, OC wants to get puck to OLD, who will pass to ORD, who will attempt to shoot. If this happens, DRW moves quickly to cover OLD, and DLW follows puck to ORD. On the faceoff, DC should try to get puck back to DRD or DRW on boards.

PLAYER MOVEMENT

PUCK MOVEMENT

87

wing covers the left wing; the center stays with the rival center; the defenseman along the faceoff line covers the rival right wing; the defensive left wing skates out toward the point, ready to react in the direction of the puck. The back defenseman remains near the goaltender.

BREAKOUT PLAYS

When a team controls the puck in its defensive zone, it must get the puck out of the zone and onto the attack as fast as possible. However, all such moves should be calculated precisely; hasty moves with the puck in the defensive zone too often result in goals for the opposition. There are set plays for getting the puck out, and the best teams execute these plays perfectly. Here are four standard breakout maneuvers, the most frequently used plays in NHL games.

1. The defenseman takes the puck behind the net and holds it there, waiting for his center to skate behind the net himself and take the puck up ice. When the center does so and starts to skate away, the defenseman must follow a

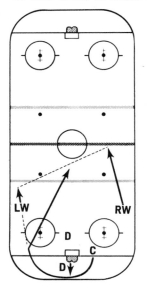

The center picks up the puck behind the net from a defenseman, skates left, passes to the left wing. Left wing takes a few strides and passes either to the center or the right wing breaking.

few strides behind in case the center loses the puck on his dribble to a fore-checking player. The center must be careful not to skate too closely to his goal. As the play takes shape, the wings skate furiously into position where they can accept a pass from the center.

2. The defenseman takes the puck behind the net and holds it there. Looking to his right and left, he decides the safest route out. Say it's to his right: he skates a few feet in that direction, then passes the puck along the boards to his right wing, who has stationed himself against the boards about halfway between the goal line and the blue line. The right wing can either skate the puck out of the zone himself, or make a precise pass to his center, who should be cruising through the middle of the ice toward the blue line. Meanwhile, the left wing, skating at the opposite side of the ice, should be a few strides ahead of the center. When the center takes the pass from the right wing, he should immediately look for his left wing and hit him with a pass. This play naturally works the other side too, with all action starting to the left if the defenseman originally determines that the safest route out is to the left.

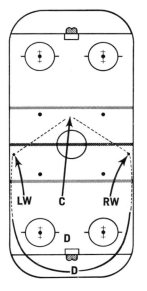

The defenseman skates either left or right from behind the net, passes off or along the boards to left or right wing, who in turn passes to breaking center or opposite wing.

89

3. The defenseman takes the puck behind the net and holds it there, weighing the situation to find the safer exit. Then he skates that way and, four or five strides out, makes a crisp pass to his center, who should be cutting across from the boards in the direction of the blue line. This pass must always be made on the inside; that is, it must be made to the side of the center nearest to the defenseman.

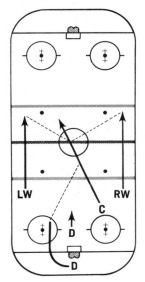

The defenseman skates out, passes to the center, who then has the option of attacking with the puck or passing it to either his left or right wing.

4. The defenseman rushes the puck up ice himself. Only a few NHL defensemen attempt this, since most of them are uncertain stickhandlers and do not think offensively. Bobby Orr of Boston is the premier offensive defenseman in hockey today. Orr starts his rushes mostly from behind his goal and is at full speed with his second or third stride. He skates out to one side, avoiding the middle at all costs, and always has another teammate trailing him in case he loses the puck. Most times Orr can sustain his rush until he reaches the far end of the ice, but even when he can't, he

still manages to get the puck out of his defensive zone and into neutral ice. Defensemen like Orr are very rare, and young players are advised not to attempt Orr-like rushes unless they are strong skaters and proficient stickhandlers. Also, when a defenseman has completed a rush, he must return to his defensive post immediately. After all, he is a defenseman first—a rusher second.

On paper, these plays seem simple. They are actually quite difficult, because the rival team doesn't stand around and permit such maneuvers without any opposition: persistent fore checkers can disrupt the best breakout plays.

KILLING PENALTIES

All teams get penalized at some time during a hockey game. Then they must play short-handed—five men against six or, in some instances, four men against six. Penalties place an extreme burden on the short-handed team; indeed, the puck may not leave the defensive zone for the duration of a penalty.

Penalty killers, therefore, are extremely valuable players. Each team must have at least three players expert at killing penalties, not including defensemen. The best penalty killers are defense-minded players with great skating ability, superior puck sense and cool heads. Indeed, penalty killers cannot be head-hunters: one man in the penalty box is bad enough; two men in the penalty box is disaster.

Penalty killers must skate hard for the period of time they are on the ice, so coaches should rotate their penalty killers with the penalty clock in mind. A coach should never keep one penalty killer on the ice for more than 75 seconds at one time. If a team happens to have four penalty killers—two sets—then the coach must try to change his penalty-killing teams about halfway through the penalty. Also, penalty killers must never be too valiant. If a penalty killer tires, he should get off the ice immediately. Tired penalty killers mean goals for the opposition.

Penalty killing begins with a strong fore-checking effort at the opposite end of the ice. The team with the player advantage will try to organize—perhaps even overorganize —its forces before skating on the attack. If a penalty killer works persistently, he can disrupt this organizational effort to the point where the attacking team will have to return and start all over again. Meanwhile, the clock ticks away— and that, after all, is what the penalty killer is trying to have it do.

However, the attacking team almost always gets the puck into its offensive zone. When this happens, the defensive team must adopt a box-zone type of defense, as diagrammed here. The four players in front of the goalie form a box, with the defensemen on opposite sides in front of the goal-

When playing one man short, the best defensive tactic is the box defense. Two defensemen are close to the goalie; two forwards are up front. This keeps the middle free.

tender and the penalty-killing forwards out closer to the blue line. They must remain in this box; two defensive players must never be in the same area. The box-zone should be as wide as possible, too. Rival players should not be permitted to penetrate the box; in fact, they must be forced as far outside the box as possible.

A rival outside the box is relatively harmless. For one thing, he has a bad angle on the goal, so he will probably not attempt a shot. He may, however, try some cute maneuver that will backfire because it was attempted in desperation. Then the penalty killers must move in and attempt to "ice" the puck whenever it is loose. If the puck is against the boards, they must attempt to tie it up there and get a faceoff.

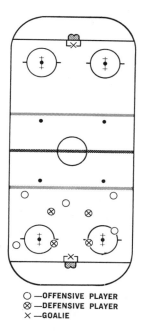

○ —OFFENSIVE PLAYER
⊗ —DEFENSIVE PLAYER
✕ —GOALIE

93

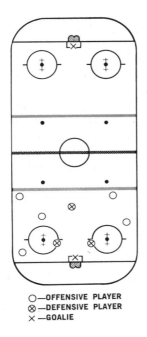

O—OFFENSIVE PLAYER
⊗—DEFENSIVE PLAYER
×—GOALIE

When a team must play two men short, that is, four against six, the best defensive maneuver is the so-called triangle. The defensemen remain in their normal positions, at both sides of the goalie. The lone penalty-killing forward stations himself about 20–25 feet in front of them. He can skate from side to side a bit, but he must never leave his area naked. Again, the penalty killers must ice the puck, freeze the puck against the boards, and, in general, do everything possible to prevent a goal. Unfortunately, the odds—six against four—are very severe.

Goaltenders must help their penalty killers too. They can hold onto the puck and create faceoffs after glove saves, and they can try to smother rebounds—or at least direct them into the corners and away from the traffic.

When playing two men short, use the triangle: two defensemen close to the goalie, one forward up front. Again, the aim is to keep the middle free.

When penalty killers get the puck around center ice, they must not be too goal-conscious. They should dribble around neutral ice with the puck, wasting the clock, and even pass it backward to a defenseman. That defenseman then can pass the puck cross-ice to his partner. The opposition usually will be ready to move in by this time, so the defenseman has only to ice the puck in order to waste more time.

Two of the best penalty killers in the NHL today are Derek Sanderson and Ed Westfall of the Boston Bruins. Sanderson is a superior puck handler and checker; Westfall is a superior defensive player—and they both are strong skaters.

Penalty killing is an art. Work at it.